AF236019

Impressum

© 2021 EmmanuelJR Asemota
Herstellung und Verlag: BoD – Books on Demand,
Norderstedt

ISBN: 978-3-7534-6141-0

DEDICATION

This Book is a Guard line,
For those going through mental pain and Physical pain.
For those in critical position in their life.

Writing this Book is a personal Therapy for me, took me 2 years after my Out of Body Experience to process how important this information is
This Book is dedicated to those passing through hard times.
For those who think they have no Reason to leave, this is for you.
There is always a Reason to leave
For those fighting Depressions after Traumatic Experience in their lives.
For those who went through Near Death Experiences
For those looking to master there Dark side and Transform them and make them work for them instead of against them.

For those looking for Answers and Enlightenment, this Book is for you.

Want you all to know that I understand How you feel, Have been through all of this myself at a very young age. All my 20cs to be honest.

This Book is dedicated to those going through Out Of Body / Traumatic Situations currently in the various

lives and almost gave up, just to inform you there is always Hope if I can make it out you can make it.

Speaking from True life Experience, so you may feel a little bit of my frustration because this is how I feel after Coma and Rehabilitation.

OUT OF BODY

When I went through my Near Death Experience I realized so many shocking fasts about life that completely change my life for Better would say and how I see things   e.g.

(1) NOTHING IN LIFE IS PROMISED

Means you can die just like that, Gone, that's the first shocking fact.

You can`t run away from Dead.

You can Die at any given time, so u have to get use to that mentality, Took me 24 Months after my Car Accident to process all the information I saw in Coma ..

If you had speak about information on How other side of the world Look, Like, most people who call you crazy for sure.

You can die anytime, so if u have the Opportunity to leave to play this Game of life, You have to play it to the fullest, You have to be the best you can be and don't lets people projects there shits on you, meanings insecurity and all of that.

Everything I Experienced was eye opening. Changes the way I view life and things, places in general

(2) CONSCIONESS- Better Known as SOUL

Consciousness is one

Consciousness is something you can only Experience

Consciousness is not something you can explain with just one word

Consciousness is Beyond Memories meaning it operates in timeless form, over there nothing like Time.

Didn't want to come back In the first place.

You Experience Past, Present and the Future at the same time (Simultaneously)

Consciousness is Beyond Physical and five sense imagination, no Beginning, no Ending, no Form, everything operates in form of Energy

People that have been through close Near Death Experience   understand what am taking about.

Energy don't die, you can only transform them.

When you die your Consciousness is 100% separated from your Body, you take another form but in physical world you are dead because your Body is dead but your Soul lives forever

Everything happens fast.

Consciousness is not Body, when you die your Soul don't die, he stays around and can only be transformed. is like Consciousness lives forever.

This information is like from other Dimension..

Your Soul stay around watching everything around itself,

He sees and feel everything around the Room, but nobody see His existence because is far away from five sense.

When I was dead for 3 days my Consciousness was able to see and feel all intentions in the Room, and staffs and Doctors and so on. The people that wishes me well and otherwise. You can scan through people in few seconds and all what they are thinking.

Nothing like Dead even if your Body dies, everything operates in Waves Frequency, you are able to just scan through everything all day like nothing happened, though I was in the movie Matrix.

After I came out of Coma, Dad had to explain to me in steps by steps about how many days the Doctors have been trying to save my life and how many

Operations have been through based on internal Brain Injuries and all that.

The Accident happened during my Break time at work..

Coming back after getting something to eat.

Recall I worked with my new Boss that day called Robin .. Was a very productive and stressful at work, but I always get the work done.

Unbelievable experience, is when I start talking about my some part of my experience with some spiritual people that went through similar situation..

They confirmed my experience was 100% True and Real, most people couldn't relate at first.

Life is not physical like most people think.

Spend a hell lot of time in bed in total and in intensive station after Coma, Only when the Doctors come to give me medication, of my Dad visiting Rather than that, they was enough silence.. So I had enough time to organized and process my true though.

at first feels like am not part of this world anymore… people probably think you are crazy because your become super sensitive to every little things, even to the cars passing by or baby crying , no music, no nothing super sensitive to this world still ..

Had enough time to process what had just happened in my life.

I was in Bed 20 Hours a day, at first it was frustrating with a lot of Pain, I was not use to this,, am extremely active person,, suddenly I don't even know even If i can walk again.

When you come out of Coma, you behave little different than usual due to too much information and drugs in the system, your need to Detox and start life from Zero in every aspect, matter of fact you will need

Rehabilitations for months to learn most things from the beginning, learn now to walk, speak, write, create, draw, eat, bath. You are completely broken.

Is like you can even loose part of your memories in so many cases.

Saw so many cases in Rehabilitation Center who never made it out normal, is like they will lose something due to the Brain injuries, Brain injuries is one of the worst

Injuries you can possible imagine specially when its bleeding internal as well for Hours or days, probability of Living normal afterword's is 9% from 100%.

(3) TIME

Time does not exist,

The concept of time is Man Made, someone made it up, you know what I mean! Dad and Doctors told me I was 3 days in Coma with a lot of effort trying to get me back to life, but for me it was just like 5mins Journey.

Future, past and present exist at the same time, Human soul is capable of a lot than people think.

When you are in your creative space you need to be careful with whom you spend time with, be careful of spending time with too many people.

Sometimes you have to figure things out yourself alone with yourself...

If you spend enough time alone, you have enough time to reflects and strategized better and efficiently- After this process you become a co-creator.. You create and design the type of live you what to leave.

Took me a little of time to get use to the normal Reality again,, some people can't come back first like I did,, or will never come back to normal even after they probably made the Accident .

First person I spoke with in Rehabilitation Center 3 months after my Accident was a man called Mr. King, call him Mr. King for a Reason best known to me,, is one of my mentor, someone I was able to speak to When I Lost my mum, was able to speak to Him during the darkest time in my Life.

Didn't want people to call me crazy so I kept most information I saw in Coma to myself , but was able to speak with Mr. king about some of it, was like 6th Dimensional type of experience, something you can probably experience under DMT is you take a lot of it,, just happens to be naturally unaware.

Our Body does not exist, and it not solid, is like we borrow them.

(4) PAIN

We only Learn through Pain or Traumatic experiences as Human.

This is why I like to use my favorite Quote:

"Came out of Coma with Super Powers"

"Self-awareness is one of the super powers"

Was able to learn a lot during those Pain period, I think that the highest pain you can ever been.

"I pushed past the pain period"

Pain are test.

They are not permanent.

Growth is painful but you need them, Changes are Painful but you need them too, nothing is as painful as staying stuck in one position for life, where you don't belong.

I use my pain to Transform and motivate myself on a Daily Basics after I realized what could have happen to me otherwise.

Pain is Real, but when can`t heal from what we never reveal.

So in Dark times, you have to learn how to use your pain to drive and motivates you, this is way I say "passed through all those pains, now feels like am illuminated or something" like am the "Truth"

In Pain period after Coma, had to use my mind as a weapon, ask about me in Trauma-Center Meidling I always pushed and pushed beyond the limits of things they told me to do, I was in a mental competition in my mind since I was in pain and physical broken , went through mental and physical pain .

Pain+ Reflection=Progress

During that pain period I said to myself Can`t let this Break me, "Instead I used that moments to empower myself"

After Coma, my physical pain was too much, had to be on 2 different pain killer for so Long,.

Couldn't sleep at night most nights for 2months...I was having so much pain that I think am having 3hours of sleep a day

During this period I had to Trick my Brain, but I understand the situation am inside. I knew I needed a stronger mindset to overcome this.

Mental physically had to start from zero again.

After years when I look back I understand my situation could had been worse than that.

Have to learn how to use my mind and focus my attention, reason why I refused to take the wheel chair the Doctor gave to me to sit for couple of months on,, I went out whenever I need to buy anything I want, I refused to obey some rules and I act based on what I wanted at time, went out to buy my meal because I couldn't eat most of their meal

Doctor told me I was among 5% of people who made out of accident like that with 60km unexpectedly, I learn a lot about me during this period I was total transformed and become more real to myself, I taped more into my creativity, I knew I had to put in the work and stay honest and true along the process if I want to get out.

When I came out of Coma, a lot of people around the Hospital when I went out to get something to eat thought I was crazy or something, could tell looking into their eyes. "Only thing that matter is how you see yourself"

The pain and Emotion I was dealing with at point in my life was too much for my age, at a point I had to speak with Therapist just to lets few things out.

Made most decision during those pain period that change my life, was a powerful moments in my life, I started writing my first official business from During Darkest times in my life, that was when I have a feeling for the first time after a long time that I found my purpose in life, what I was made to do

Pain+ Reflection=Progress

(5) INTENSIVE-STATION

For those who don't understand what Intensive station means, is a place where they put patient after Coma for weeks or months without outside world contact, because they are still sensitive to the environment. Spend total of 8 weeks there.

Was the place I started studying about my "super power"

I always tell people I came out coma with "super power"

When I went back to work and school people that calling me Wave.

I know if I can make it pass through this, it will make all the difference.

After Dad explain what happened to me, couldn't believe, took me months after to realize.

Went through several operation.

When I look at myself in the mirror, couldn't believe the person I saw, lost almost 15Killos.

I said to myself over and over again, am not going to give up.

Started writing the list of things am going to change in my life if I come out of the Hospital, if I can walk again, was a critical point in my life. Wasn't sure if am going to make it through, but I believe strongly looked nothing like a person I use to recognized. I focused more on the inside, mind you this is a new process for me in life, but my Brain understand I have to do it, I have no option.

Had a quick recovery in general the doctor said, was not until I went to Rehabilitation I realized my situation was way better than most if not all. Doctor told My Dad I was supposed to be on the wheel chair for months, but I refused. Started going out myself, even when I was physically broken, but my mind was not had to be on medication still for 1 year, when I look back I understand the reason why the doctor said I was a fighter, I was among the chosen one.

(6) REHABILITATION

Is a big part of my Post Trauma Treatment?
Place where you go to right after intensive station to ensure your mental and physical states of mind are in good conditions. I undergo several Therapy section a day. 9 different Therapy a day for 7weeks. I did tremendously fine in the Therapy sections, guess I couldn't wait to share my ideas with the world. One of which group Therapy where I come to know this young lady called Patricia, she had a car accident like me, and only different was she was the one driving. And she go partly hit by a train passing by her village because she lives in the country side and got transfer to Rehabilitation center in Vienna city where am from where I meet her. She ask my name? Almost every time when we have group therapy together, at first thought it was a joke than I realized woooooow not at all the doctor told me she hard like a permanent loss of memories and she will have a hard time recalling people's names or what she read, worst is she is a student of university

of Graz and Alost in her final year, she is looking fine and can talk normal but only different is she can't recall that much.

Remember the first day I introduced myself to her, and after 24 she ask in a normal way again,, Hey what your name, and I told her.. This happened A lost every day before I left

Rehabilitation Center, matter of facts I meet her there and I left her there and couple others people, That was when I realized I was extremely lucky, I appreciate every moment and every day and my peace of mind become a daily goal for me, probably the reason why I leave like is my last day till today. Am more grateful till today for all those experiences, at that point I understand I have a "Bigger purpose to serve"

Something bigger than me, shout all the Therapist in Rehabilitation-Center Meidling during Rehabilitation Period I was in 4th floor and 3rd floor was people after accident without legs, at that point I realized this guys

Are going to be on a wheel-chair for the rest of their lives

(7) CHANGES

Everything happened at its own divine time.

Everything has its own season.
So if you are having a bad time in your life and business right now, the good news is dark times don't last forever , you always need to have that mind set that's the good news I guess.
Time & Changes are so important in our life, you become who are as a result of how you use and manage your time.
One of The key to personal success in my opinion is a result of how we use our time. You can`t stop time
So as well you can`t change it, so all you could do with them is to learn how to manager them, Time is our Asset, Time is not forever, we have to make use of it now.
Time Build your life.
Our life as Human is on Timer, you will leave this planet when the time comes.
We become who we become based on how we use our 24Hours.

Make use of your time wisely.

Common sense is not common anymore

Time is powerful

Hope is good, but plan is better.

Dream and hopes don't change your life, but plan does.

If you don't control your time, other people would

(8) VISION

After this experience I promised to be myself everyday till I die, figured that out that it's expensive to be someone else you're not.

Imagine been someone you're not every day for a year.

Also promised to stay true to my Vision and Purpose in life.

Building something iconic takes time, also have to teach myself to stay cool, calm and collective no matter what.

Sometimes is good to have a vision than without one.

People have this need to be right all the time, I personally pick what is true not what is right, been perfect does not always change things.

Your pay the price for everything including your vision, when I realized I have a vision and mission, I couldn't sleep a day without inspiration finding me, if you have a Vision you need some amount of focus, is really essential to be focus in other to manifest you what.

The prices you pay for getting your vision across is sometimes unfair, not cheap but you have to do it.

Most times you have to pay the cost to be the Boss, sometimes the cost is everything and you have to be able to be fine with that, given everything away you love for the moment for greater purpose, losing relationship and friends is normal when your moving up, at first was depressing but got used to it with time.

Don't make people make you feel less about yourself for having a vision, because maybe they don't have one.

Vision make me leave in the middle of difficulties you can never imagine, reason why is because am 100% sure sunshine is coming, I know a day is coming will laugh it all off and thank myself for been brave.

Vision is inside all of us as a Human, you just have to find them, mostly it's something personal, First Vision than Money, you can`t do both at the same time, impossible.

Intelligence increase through what we learn with the help of skills.

Success comes easy, he actually going to come searching for you if you have a real vision.

Success is not luck, so next time you see please don't tell me how lucky I am, I just chose to make it look easy, have been positioning myself since the universe knowns when, 3 years or something more. Work hard for this even if I keep myself so simple with it.

Luck don't exist, even when it look like one.

Everyone what to be successful until I told the "prices I have to pay"

Too many sacrifices along the way to success,

Do anything for my Vision.

(9) MEDITATION

Meditation means Listening.

I personally feel like as Human we have to listen more.

Meditation change my life post Out of Body Experience for better.

Meditation is one of the important aspect of my life till today, will never trade that for nothing.

Meditation is most important aspect of prayer.

Your dream is reveal to you when you are in silence, not when you are talking, don't forget distraction is everywhere in the world, so is always important to have a moment of silence in a day for yourself , just you and you alone, listening to what the universe have in response to your prayer and wises .

"Your Heart can`t see" because "eyes have so many distractions.

Meditation helps reduce my Anxiety after Rehabilitation.

Is like in life you have to fight for your peace of mind, peace of mind is important in career and life general now, I always value them , will pay any price for my peace of mind.

Don't care how much am going to get payed, if I can`t feel good and sleeping good at night, am not going to do the business deal, I just how I function, am all about building something from nothing to make it iconic care less about fast money , am

Long term thinker, and vision make that possible.
Hope one day some of you we realized how important Meditation can be, so many answers can come to you in the state of meditation, try it.

(10) CANNABISPLANT🍁🖤

Cannabis Help me a lot.
Been using Cannabis-plant for couple of years now with breaks in between. But after my out of Body experience I was in pain even do when I took pain killers.
Cannabis-Help Reduce my pain, remember smoking a lot of Cannabis in Rehabilitation center, all the doctor knows I use it, mind you at that point I was still on medication. I used Cannabis as a Therapy because of my physical which made me couldn't sleep for days, so had to turn to my best friend at that time 🍁

Think the general population has to cultivate the habit of using plants and not miss using them, at the point in my life Cannabis help me sleep better with less problem.
Ask anybody that has been through that level of pain, they will tell you pain is real .Imagine you lost

15killos suddenly? And you have to eat yogurt and corn flecks and put in milk for Hours before eating it because all your jaw are total broken and you need 6months till 8 months to eat proper food, take time getting use to eating normal again, remember that feeling.

I understand that people questioned my personality in the hospital when they find out I used cannabis plant, but I careless about them knowing that part of me, in my mind is just Medication and I treat it like such till date.

I Respect and chose to use Cannabis Responsible and I will advise that for all user. Always hide it from kids, even my Dad is aware about my use, guess I was shocked when he notice my Love for the plant, but with time was able to prove to him am responsible with it.

Money can't buy Emotional intelligent, no matter how much money, some people remain ignorant about some things or area of life, to the

point where sometimes I act less intelligent so I can ignore there inaccuracy and Hypocrisy of people, just because something doesn't work for you does not mean it wouldn't work for someone else even if your guys are twin brother doesn't matter is still the same rule. The amount of ignorance in the world make me speechless so many times, to the point where I ask myself! Should ignorance be consider a disease in our modern age?

(11) PROGRESS

People call it success but truly I like to use the word Progress.

Success is not like most successful themselves make you think.

Success is personal.

Success is far away from luck, to my own understanding is like you fail your way to success, "Knowledge is the key to freedom" the

"Knowledge of truth shall set you free"

Have tried so many things,

Worked in small and big organization, when through so many traumatic experiences like losing someone close to you. My coma experience was the last point, was the moment my life change. I started tapping into another universe and I love the struggle more, feel in love more with my vision and the process even when it was painful, but I feel good knowing every single day am working forwards my Goal & Dream.

Laugh when some people thing success is a coincident, matter of facts you have to plan for success nothing coincident about that, but so many things will happened a lot the way, you just have to be flexible like my dad advise me first time he had am going to be Entrepreneur.

After Coma, I took 100% ownership of my life
I stop blaming people, I start blaming myself, a very interesting game to play because now you feel responsible for your life and for every action you take, imagine living in a world where nobody hold you accountable for what you do, it will surely be mess.

Started making touch decisions that I normally wouldn't make for long time.
People in my environment sometimes don't understand the reason way I behave the way I do, and is not my job to explain, all you have to do is to look at my story, maybe you will understand my drive and where am coming from and where am going, is like there is light inside me and am following

that light or voice inside of me and I don't care what people think or call it, feels almost stupid not following that voice, that the zone I go when I need to make any touch decision.

All I ever wanted is to be Successful and still remain kind and generous on my terms, because deep inside me no matter how successful am going to become, I believe I have a beautiful and a generous side.

Sometimes when I look back I laugh about the past me, is like the new me recognized the old me, in past and current situation in my life.

Use to remember how I act when I feel angry in some situation, now I figured those aspect of my life out.

People call me Arrogant, I call myself healthy confident, no matter wish label people try to give me at a point didn't listen to them because it's easy to make that stops you, I know who I am and where am going and who am trying to become in long term .

Please don't be Ignorant and Arrogant is a big turn off.

"Be careful of judging people when you don't know the full story"

Am cool with trying not to impress nobody but me

(12) ENTERPRENEURSHIP

Entrepreneurship is not made for everybody, crazy why people can`t play the game right.

So many depressing moments but you always have to fight through no matter what, I believe in my vision even when nobody believe in me.

One thing I don't like in business world is not getting what I want, most average people couldn't believe how much you have to sacrifice to get what you what., Have you ever sacrifice yourself!, and everything you loved!., buying cars, going to clubs because most of your friends did, Buying expensive sneakers, and going to holiday all of that.

Seems unfair at first, but when I spoke to a successful business man they all went through that stage too where they can`t afford to buy thing the loved to buy because they are running the company with their private money, but the results is going to be crazy years later.

So I said to myself fuck everyone else since most of my friends are not business minded, need to make new friends like me, they don't understand the concept of entrepreneur so I think sharing my knowledge with them is a waste of time, because I feel like giving someone information when they are not ready can be a waste of time, they will beg for it when the time come.

You have to separate yourself from small minded people, with no vision, have been dreaming of this all my life, I finally meet the game I enjoy playing the best, been through so many insult situation and unforgiven moments in my career but I forgive myself, take it like a learning experience, most people can`t sacrifices or stay years without Dripping and getting what they want instantly, everybody want it instantly and forget about long term while long term is the real wealth.

Entrepreneur=Artist
Entrepreneur=Artist

Wave Cbd is the name of my first Startup Company, at first it was an idea, than Business now vision, is bigger than me.

Can`t go to place I use to, or do things I use to while doing this, so many unforgiven and unforgettable moment at the beginning.

So crazy and so true, that sometimes I ask myself where I get this strength from doing this, staying days without eating because I had just paid for something for the company, ask myself why am I so patient, never been like this before to the point where I do anything just to make my vision come to live .

Rather die as a respected person than like a coward. I stayed true to my core value, been patient though be a hell lot maybe the Coma experience though me a lot of patient too as a person, help shape my character would say. Know am learning new business skills every now and then.

I develop a code of life, and I will die by this code, I hope you find your code one day, reason why is because if I don't, I won`t sleep better at night. Will never compromised for money or any jobs or business deal, I understand is not good for my mental health, that not how I started the vision.

My mental health is the most important for me while doing business, they are just things I can`t give away or do no matter how, my moral and core value is hard to change those things about me and am not willing to trade that for nothing in this world, no matter how far I go or how success I become in my career

Entrepreneur=Artist

(13) SIGMA-PERSONALITY TYPES

Sigma personality types.

Most people want to know the reason why I behave the way I do, they want to know that wrong with me, they want to know what my personality type look like?

Sigma personality type, mind you this took me years after years studying my personality and people close to me in my family they say the same thing too I finally came to the conclusion that have been like that for years, at first though something is wrong with my personality for years till found out I was acting right to my nature.

Sigma is the same as Alpha personality.

Most people complain to my dad growing up, why don't he gives a fuck?.

People tell me several times, that its seems like I naturally don't care.

Truth is, is not that I don't care.

I focus on my ideas and though, so sometimes am blind to the World and sometimes I pay attention, just that I pay less attention to things am less passionate about, only if I feel the need than I pay attention, but am careful with it, Truth is, that is my natural state of not reacting to external world, I just pick what I want and leave the rest

When I study myself would say it's the right question to ask, they want to know if I naturally don't care or if am arrogant.
Growing up till now I have a take it or leave it attitude to life in general, towards women and everything.
Sigma type like me are have the same personality traits like Alpha, only different is they chose to leave out the social circle and I love that about me, wouldn't trade that for nothing .
Took me years to realized that am Sigma type to the fullest, when I see people fight over things I honestly don't even want makes me laugh, in my mind am thinking leftovers, don't want it anyways, because I know what I want .
Sigma like social life, but love the in depend.

I personal value my peace of mind more than most people could imagine about me or more than average person, I have my rules, never leave life based on what people think. Remember before I was 18 years old was already thinking something is surely wrong with my personality, asked myself in several occasion even early before 15years, I was just something different, asked myself why am I not just like others , took me lot years later to understand my true personality ..

Sigma personality are not that so much in the world generally, a good example of a sigma type is Kobe Bryant, watch video of Kobe and watch how he speaks and how he acts.

I don't complain

I hate bitching around like a baby, I take the consequent of my actions, and I learn when to involved my energy , mostly I don't care what people around me thing about an idea or anything, If am feeling good about it am doing it period, can say that about my personality so far .

"Am not arrogant"

"Am just confident"

Not to be arrogant, I personally don't respect most people, maybe because of things have seen from childhood growing up, and takes a lot to earn my respect as a person, and to keep it.

People get mad or confused when they get around me and see the standards I demand from people around me and myself is high, most people have low standards so they may get jealous.
I understand some people frustration and pain, but I will never respect them like I said, I do my own thing and dance to my own beat. Imagine you needing the validation of nobody to feel complete! Think about that for a second, you can even meditate on it if you want.

Could be generous unexpectedly sometimes, but would like to look at myself as authentic and confident human, nobody can make me feel good or less good, "I move when I move" "I roll when I roll" Took me years to admit and accept myself.
You can`t fake sigma personality.

I personally can`t be bothered.

Have got so many things to do or fix, all I do is face my Mission and Vision and I try all I could to stay out of the Attention of others.

Am not attention seeker.

I stay away from the lime light even if my personality, attitude and Nature attract others to me, is like the less I try from my heart the more attraction I got, even if people can see I naturally don't care about the attention.

You can ask my family about my personality, I remember been so angry at my friends in school and our neighbors, and been angry at the society at large growing up, because they don't understand how I work, was so angry at my community because most kids was not just like me, and it was clear to see, even when I was kid my dad started telling me at a young age how different I am, so I understand this is not a joke. Could smell this kids are not just like me.

Have my own unique way of getting things done"
I do things in a different way because that who I am
"Even if I don't try, people think I do"
I stay in my own space and chase my Dream, I see no competition, only person am in competition with is myself.

BONUS-POINT

Everything has its price, and limitation, so you have to be willing to understand the roots of your problems. But Sometimes you just have to roll the dice and make things happened, so but in other to make things happen you need e.g.
Plan, Vision and changes.
Enduring pain period is Real and important, if not you will think the pain are forever, when I look at my life and at the Vision and opportunity I created around me due to enduring the pain, is amazing, but took a hell lot of Hard and smart work, no two ways to it, had to position myself for the right time to come for years.

This is the person I become, no going back for me. During the darkest time in my life didn't know I was doing this, you have to turn inside and find out about some questions only you have answers to, and I completely ignore the world around me for a while just to get those answers.

Study your personality type and how you function so you wouldn't go again yourself as a person.

Social Networking is a Trading abilities, Social abilities to sell.

Dark times are test, you have to go inside and search for question you needed answer for years, you need to go inside words to find out about your Super-Power or true self or even solution to your problems or even Stat up a new business.

Dark times are powerful, you can lets them break you or make you, so if you made it out of Dart times with Super-Power nothing can break you anymore, but you have to obey the laws, don't know how to explain this, most people who made it out of dark times become unstoppable, master your Dark side now.

But you have to stay Honest to the process, Endurance is one of the key.

Organizing and Administrative skills or ability are important to get to the next level, "Everything has its prices" "nothing in life is free"